True

True

PAUL JEFFCUTT

THE **BLACK SPRING**
PRESS GROUP

First published in 2025
An Eyewear Publishing book, The Black Spring Press Group
Maida Vale, London W9,
United Kingdom

Typeset with graphic design by Edwin Smet

isbn 978-1-915406-49-1

BLACKSPRINGPRESSGROUP.COM

Printed and bound in Great Britain by Clays Ltd, Elcograf S.p.A.

Dedicated to the late Ciaran Carson.

Ciaran Carson led the Writers' Group
at the Seamus Heaney Centre in Belfast,
where all the poems in this collection
were first read and discussed.

The poems collected here were stimulated by real-life stories
I encountered in a variety of media. They are not 'found poems'.
The real-life story has instead provided a launch point for the poem.
Ciaran Carson christened them 'discovered poems'.
This collection brings together my discovered poems.

Paul Jeffcutt has won thirty-three awards for poetry
in competitions in Ireland, the UK and the USA.
He has two previous collections: *The Skylark's Call*,
Dempsey & Windle (2020) and *Latch*, Lagan Press (2010).
He is widely published in literary journals and anthologies.
www.pauljeffcutt.net

CONTENTS

COMPASS *

Take the metalled road
that traverses the treeless spine
of the farthest inhabited island,
past the Final Checkout
for frozen and shelved goods
and Bobby's Bus Shelter
with curtains, sofa and books.
Ascend the peaty heath
of mouse-eared chickweed
and arctic roundwort
above cliffs and stacks chocked
with guano and raucous gannets,
as the spume-flecked grey ocean
incessantly surges and falls.
Climb onward to Saxa Vord,
great skuas dive-bombing
the Cold War radar station
instead of Fencers and Bears.
Brace at the beacon
against a keen northerly
that once rose to 177mph,
before the equipment blew away,
and wait
for a rocket
to the Moon.

* a note for this poem is found in the Notes section in the back

WRITING EXERCISES *

Abbot's piss
turd of prince

Quicklime bath
fortnight's steep

Scud pelt
stretch on herse

Pippin cords
flay the hide

Pounce and prick
gather a quire

Trim quill
dip in ink

EAST IRELAND: A COLONIAL NOTEBOOK *

Rain set in.

Marched from Newry to Rathfriland, distance fourteen miles.
The first part of the route I did not see, being asleep
on Major Henley's elephant. Arrived Mayobridge at midday,
where I located my horse. The road then tolerably good,
interspersed with streams and banyan trees. Comfort
and cleanliness are little observed in these parts.
Found quarters in Rathfriland, water good
and plenty of supplies for a battalion.
Building great temples and drinking illicit whiskey
prevails among the populace. The country about,
one continued prospect of dark, rocky hills.
Killed a snake in my sleeping room.

Marched to Katesbridge, distance eight miles.
A precipitous descent into jungle,
sighted leopard, apes and buffalo
but I could not obtain a clear shot.
Our native guide twice lost his way
so we did not reach the river Bann until sunset.
Across the muddy water a wretched place,
not above thirty dwellings built in a square
by way of defence. A six-pounder
would demolish the whole in ten minutes.

Marched to Castlewellan, distance twelve miles.
The coldest morning so far, my feet were near frozen
in the stirrups and my horse sank to his withers
crossing the river Bann. The road beyond mostly sound
but in places steep and stony. Proceeded through land in crop
of sugar cane and rice. Castlewellan, with a fine bazaar,
appears capable of supplying a large camp.

Weather cool, light rain.

FLAT WHITE *

When you've pondered the beans,
arabica, typica, robusta,
from sustainable plantations
untainted by captive labour
in Guatemala, Kenya and Brazil,
shipped under responsible flags
and trucked to this emporium
in zero-emission electrics
driven without swearing
by uniformed migrants
on guaranteed-hours contracts,
then chosen the receptacle,
china, glass, fully-recyclable paper,
number of shots, type of water,
mix of steam and milky froth,
cow's, goat's, soy or almond,
taken a naughty macaroon
or furtive slab of carrot cake,
additive and palm oil free,
to your table of repurposed wood
with salvaged steel legs
and plonked your well-toned
12,000-steps-a-day behind
onto the ethnic-cushioned bench –
you recline against the wall
of exposed red bricks and mortar,
glance at the dishevelled man
slumped face-down two tables away
no cup or plate before him.
A shake of your head,
you check your inbox.

MORNING

Near Elephant and Castle
eight lie in cardboard
bunched at the foot of
a block of flats

Teenagers yawn
jape and blather
in the cemetery
of sleepers

Hoar frost glistens
drain pipes seep
one of St Mungo's
stops and asks

DUE

Tibulus the freed-man of Venustus
wrote with an iron stylus
in lamp-blackened beeswax
coated on a tablet of fir
to Gratus the freed-man of Spurius,
one hundred and five denarii he owed
for merchandise sold and delivered to him
in Londinium six days before the Ides of January.

One thousand nine hundred and fifty seven years later
the tablet was found, preserved in mud,
as foundations were dug in the City.
The beeswax gone,
his debt remained
etched in wood.

COUNTING ON CHANCE *

He lays Adam Smith's roman beak
on top of the Royal visage
until one hundred blue noses
rub together in profile.
Gathering up the notes,
he snaps on a rubber band
and pockets the stash.

A northern colliery village,
the pit closed, then the shops –
young ones to the city,
the remainder hanging on,
obstinate as hillside terraces,
back-to-back with loan sharks
and bronchial memories.

Hood raised,
he prowls thin streets.
Nobody about –
he tosses the cash
to the pavement
and walks on.

PILGRIM *

Mud slops and clutches
the girl's leather shoes,
they were grandma's best –
one foot slides to the toe,
the other pulls from the heel.
She stumbles,
shifts papa's blue bag
across tender shoulders,
plods on.

After her hidey-hole
she'd searched the street.
Nobody there
except the quiet ones
lying awkwardly.

She flops onto the bag,
gathers mama's coat at her neck.
Battered cars lurch between craters,
bearded men jeer,
two lads on a motorbike
poke and slap her.
She shakes her head,
the hissing in her ears
stops for a moment.

Three struggle from the muck,
two boys and a woman.
No-one speaks.
Remote eyes meet.
It's time to move on.

BREAKFAST IN KUTUPALONG *

Half a dozen skinny kids
squat around a tin pot
preparing the rice ration,
their tiny earth-floored hut
of bamboo and blue plastic sheet
shudders as the rains lash
these cramped border hillsides
to rust-brown streams of ooze.

Down the waterlogged trail
our lorry stalls,
laden with sacks of rice
from an Atlantic island
no stranger to damp or want.
Kalim takes the wheel,
guns the flooded engine
and steadies a course
to the sea of ragged shelters.

RECKONING *

Black turnips, rotten cabbages, dung –
we hurl them with zeal.
The flesh of the enchained
turns dark as their hearts.

May the Lord free you from sin,
he barks, crozier raised.
All cower save one
who looses a stream of piss.

Pikemen stride forward,
buttons glinting on blue tunics.
Muttering incantations,
the damned stagger into the cage.

He lifts a hand to the heavens
and our great bell begins to toll.
A turnkey makes fast the bars,
pikemen grasp the rope.

On a wave of raucous cheers,
the cage sways to the campanile.
Then the auld one screams –
hellbine, devil's hair, deadman's lace.

OBSERVANCES

Slicked with oil of spikenard,
cased in alabaster,
entrusted to St John,
Charlemagne, Pope Leo III,
looted from Rome
by the Duke of Bourbon,
exposed at Antwerp,
Besançon, Charroux,
Hildesheim, Le Puy,
and eaten by St Birgitta:
but the foreskin was fake,
avowed Leo Allatius,
head of the Papal Library,
for it had ascended,
alongside the Redeemer,
and formed a Ring of Saturn.

THE PROPHET *

Three chickens,
two cats &
a cryptologist
take a pilgrim path
through great ravines
to the last cove
of a soulless land.

The cats crouch
to escape the wind.
The chickens peck
the dark sand.
He screeches
at foaming waves,
brandishing a spoon.

MONTEREY PINE

Worshipped by the Ohlone,
you stood at the margin of spirit worlds –
beside healing waters replete with otters, perch and sea
lions,
a roost for yellow-billed magpies, tiger owls,
downy woodpeckers and red-shafted flickers
beneath the great, dancing sky.
You watched conquistadors plunder the land,
missionaries capture souls by the sword
and The Man with No Name become Mayor.

Sun rises
Wind stirs
Rain falls

THE PLAYLIST

Dictator, CIA Agent,
Chief of Military Intelligence,
US-funded gun-runner,
Director of Paramilitary Death-squads,
cocaine-trafficker and opera-lover,
General Manuel Noriega
took sanctuary in The Vatican Embassy, Panama,
from a US invasion force
under General Colin Powell
launched by President George Bush,
a rehearsal for Iraq.

Surrounding the Embassy with military hi-fi,
American troops blasted him:
Led Zeppelin, Megadeth, Guns N' Roses,
Iron Maiden, AC/DC, Black Sabbath,
salvo after salvo at ear-splitting volume
bombarded non-stop day and night.

The Embassy reverberated:
windows cracked, walls throbbed.
El Nuncio strutted air-guitar.
Noriega prayed.

CHUAN-PU *

Li Liangwei blusters
in sharp suit and red tie,
flanked by black-shaded
black-suited bodyguards,
snips the shiny ribbon
of a hotel in Shenzhen
reciting poetry
by Mao Zedong.

Li mimics his lookalike
from satellite TV news.
His agent tells him to blink
and flap his hands more.
Li does not use Twitter.

'The sky is high
the clouds are light
wild geese flying south
are out of sight.'

THE ROMANOVS *

Fled the deadly Ural cellar
with an air-freight oligarch
who resuscitated Rasputin,
poisoned with cyanide,
declared him Archbishop.

They reign in the Kremlin,
a duplicate gilded palace
on a private Pacific island,
domes glinting over palms
as peasants till and gripe.

Lenin returned to exile
in Zurich by train,
Stalin didn't drive
an ice axe into
Trotsky's head.

FIXER *

It's fluid
electric

Some appear
others disappear

An acid bath
the cropping out

It will happen
trust me

VISIT NAGASAKI *

The Portuguese were first.
We traded silks
for copper and silver.

Their preachers roused peasants.
We crushed the rebellion
and banished all.

The Dutch came.
We consigned them to a trading post,
storehouses rich in books and sugar.

We built a causeway to the West:
docks, ships, aircraft,
the machinery of empire.

Munitions factories at the limit,
conscript housewives
and schoolboys.

A gap in the clouds,
one aeroplane.
Hibakusha rise.

BOG MEN *

Wavy brown hair
slicked with resin
Mediterranean Pine
held at the nape
in a gold clasp

Bronze amulet
mounted with copper
Fox fur armband
Leather wristband
Neat clipped beard
Manicured fingers
Severed nipples
Fractured skull
Disembowelled

Quare
Cursed
Croghan
Clonycavan
Lost at home

IRON ANNIVERSARY

Old Conley wakes to cries
stabs scrawny long-johned legs
into shit-stained old suit trousers
held at the waist with baler twine
drags on hobnailed boots
frayed flannel shirt and once-green jersey
smeared with dregs from countless feeds
scrapes a greasy cap onto a grizzled head
kicks open the door to the stinking yard.
Rooks scatter and caw above the sycamore
his chained collie bitch stretches and yawns
filthy water dribbles over battered concrete
oozing between clods and spilled hay
as bullocks roar and clatter in the corrugated barn.

Hunching against the sleet that spears from Blue Hill
he slings the mildewed heel of a loaf at the collie
she snatches it from the dirt and gulps it whole
pads close and licks his hand. He howls
clamps his great gnarled paws around her neck
heaves the collie into the air
her frantic legs tearing against him
forces scarred thumbs into warm matted fur
squeezing her whining white throat
ever tighter
to stop the screams
of his young wife and son
tearing down the rickety stairs
and away.

CURTAIN BOAR *

All sorts he's covered:
downy and pink, smooth as an ear,
warted and reeking of the ditch.
Wains by the thousands,
curious tails and handy snouts,
squabbling for the teat –
eight weeks and they're away,
never the merest glance.

Down the yard, a skiff of rain,
the lane-way to the foreshore
and the furthest lands.
His house gets smaller.

ESSENCE

She removes her coat
stretches back
breath by breath
smears petals steeped in fat
the warm gland of a tiny deer
and grease from a whale's gut
across each wrist
behind her knees
in the crook of her elbows
beneath each ear.

She stills herself
flickering by the fire
I'll eat him alive.

WOODPECKERS

A wondrous drumming
alerts the nature reserve
to a pair of rare visitors,
great spotted woodpeckers
excavating a hole in a tree
to breed and rear young.

The birds have chosen a site
rife with grey squirrels
tempted to raid the nest
for a feast of chicks or eggs,
a patch of scrubby woodland
frequented daily by men
who meet for casual sex
while unleashed dogs play.

THE HARPSICHORD TUNER *

Long delicate fingers clasp the hammer,
his elegant head leans across the keys
and auburn curls slip forward.
Noticing my glance, he looks away with soft brown eyes.
'Please forgive me, Frau Beethoven,
my hair has need of dressing.'
'Not at all, Herr Fischer, you have such fine locks.'
'I would wear a periwig, if I had the means.'
'Fear not, dear sir. Johann will increase your stipend forthwith.
But I must implore you, do not spend it on a wig.
And please call me Maria.'
'I am truly grateful for your kindness, Maria.
All will certainly be spent on meat or wood for the fire.
Since father died, our situation is injurious.'
'May he rest in peace, Gottfried.
I fathom your woe most sincerely. My first-born was buried
not one year past.'
'My deepest condolences, Maria. You have been sorely tested.'
'We both have, dear sir. Life is filled with sorrow.'
'That is indeed true, dear lady.
But we must endeavour to turn circumstances to our advantage.'
'Gottfried, would you take a glass of schnapps with me?'
'Thank you kindly, but I cannot while my task remains.'
'Nonsense. A tot will speed your hand and hone your ear.'
'But Kantor Beethoven will shortly return to inspect my work.'
I offer him the chair beside me
and collect two glasses from the cabinet.
Johann would linger at the tavern until his coin was all spent
and stumble home cursing and carousing.
'Thank you, Maria, you are most hospitable.'
'My pleasure, Gottfried, you are a tender man.'

ALBIES PHANTOM *
— *for Justice Albie Sachs*

Without me to steer it,
the indigo arm of his suit flutters and swerves.
He's speaking on truth and reconciliation again –
that hand an anchor, trapping his notes to the desk,
this sleeve a flag of passion,
the vacant space that's rightly mine.

Long after the car bomb in Mozambique,
he's told the secret agent wants to confess.
At the Commission, a chance meeting.
The agent timidly makes to shake,
I scream
'You've already taken me, you bastard.'
Albie pauses, then proffers –
'Here, I have another one.'

HABANA CABARET *

The guts of a grand hotel
stuffed with 50's Americana:
yellow-finned Chevrolet convertible
and chromed maw of Buick sedan,
the dance floor – a bulging glitterballed tongue,
Cuban octet stuck in the throat,
sharp white suits, red bow-ties,
swinging out 'Somewhere Over the Rainbow'
to tables scattered like spittle.

In place of Lucky Luciano and the mob,
ageing white hands rent fresh-faced natives.
A curtain call and the DJ starts, with *reggaeton* –
wrinkled, flat-footed squeezes shake their heads.
Jinetero waves across the floor to *jinetera* –
sparkling, they join in ecstatic dance
and return to be yoked
to their owners.

BAGGAGE *

Picked up and let go,
not even a wave,
I'm left in the shadows again.
You trust we'll be reunited
but I'll bob down the track,
under the radar and away.

Standby or red-eye,
further the better for me –
with holdall, rollercase and drinks
beneath wispy coconut fronds.
A week without your sweaty palm,
what bliss

SLEEP RESEARCH

Huddled around embers
in a smoke-blackened cave,
early humans slept –
half their brain on the alert
for predators.

In a strange bed,
modern humans regress...
prowling the corridors
of every hotel –
a clouded leopard,
dire wolves,
the great black bear.

THE KNOWLEDGE *

Our feet will provide:
they stand the load,
wade the river,
carry the child,
tiptoe for berries,
clamber to spy the land,
stalk the spoor,
troop the meat to camp
and take us on our way.

Many seasons we've roamed,
each scored on the staff
my father handed to me.
He tramped through desert,
loped beside wolves,
slithered across sea ice,
tracked every beast.

Build a fire,
paint me with ochre,
prepare deer loin,
red berries and sweet-water.
I'll tell you about the snow bear
and black serpents of the trees.

SAGA *

Einar oily-tongue
son of Thorir the silent
brother of Harald fair-hair
and Olaf the white took Ragnhilda
daughter of Amund wall-eye had three sons
Thord half-foot Gudred most-beard and Sigurd
the stout. One midwinter Einar caught tidings Olaf
Bjarn hook-tooth and his housecarls would war him
he parleyed with Steinhoff the low and Thorsten cod-biter
rode forth with his sons and twenty men to settle the matter
at the place of stones Bjarn offered him single combat
they clashed long with sword and axe
till Einar severed Bjarn's neck a mighty strike
Olaf the white gave Solveig his daughter to Thord for wife
they made up the quarrel Einar hung Bjarn's head
from his mount's crupper set for home in celebration
as he spurred the horse Bjarn's tooth pierced his calf
the wound sprung with large swelling his sons laid him
in the hall at Orphir gave sacrifice three hermits
but the great warrior chief Einar oily-tongue
went in fever to his death.

ABANDONED ALONG LA RUTA DE DON QUIJOTE

A dead falcon,
olive stones, single mattress
ripped, large black boot, carcass
of a washing machine, goat turds,
wide-brimmed wickerwork hat,
one bicycle wheel with broken spokes,
a book on chivalry, whose name
I do not care to recall,
stamped *Biblioteca de Toledo*.

PASSAGE *

He cuts the loaf.
She fills my bowl,
thin potato broth.
We swallow,
candles flutter,
no-one speaks.

The jarvey knocks.
Gather coat
and carpet bag.
We clasp.
Tilt my hat
to hide my eyes.

Pulled aboard
the jaunty car,
he squeezes my hand.
Wave until
the last house
disappears.

His skewbald
clippity-clops
the turf lands
below Nephin,
our car judders
and pitches.

The early train
for Queenstown
full to overflow.
In the luggage van,

surrounded
by keepsakes.

The landlord's
agent lunches
at Castle Gore,
soaks weary bones
in Kilcullen's
Seaweed Baths.

Belching smoke,
the mighty ship
rounds the point,
four funnels,
prow the height
of our mountain.

Seven pounds,
fifteen shillings
and ninepence.
Money owed.
Third class ticket.
One way.

CUSTOMS *

Mary makes the tea,
sets the pot on the hob,
slathers still-warm scones
with butter and damson jam,
plucks and fills two mugs,
stirs in a slip of milk
and heads for the parlour.

A red and white barrier
blocks the door to the hall,
the guard inspects her tray.
Export tariffs are due
on butter, flour and milk
before husband Pat
can take a bite.

FRUIT CAKE

Mix flour, sugar, butter, currants, sultanas, lemon & orange peel,
almonds, cloves, nutmeg and brandy.

Coat a deep rectangular tin with melted lard and line it
with a double layer of baking parchment.

Spoon in the mixture. Bake at 300 degrees Fahrenheit for 3 ¾ hours.
Leave to cool and turn out on a wire rack.

Wrap securely in waxed paper and store in an airtight tin
decorated with a globe and swallows, with *Huntley & Palmers*,
All the World Over and *By Appointment to His Majesty The King*
emblazoned on the lid.

Convey by wagon and locomotive from the bakery in Reading
to Cardiff Docks.

Sail to Madeira, South Trinidad, Simonstown, Melbourne,
Lyttleton, Port Chalmers and Cape Evans.

Disembark alongside flags, timber, weapons, fuel, instruments,
sledges, hardware, stoves, tents, alcohol, snowshoes, tobacco,
dry goods, skis, preserves, sleeping bags, clothing, 33 dogs,
25 men and 17 ponies.

'Outside the door of the tent remains a wild scene of whirling drift.
It seems a pity but I do not think I can write more...'

Found unopened at Cape Adare, Antarctica, 106 years later.

Still edible.

CONCERNING THE FIRST VOYAGE OF
R L STEVENSON WITH HIS FATHER *

Huge sea tossing the fore-deck,
ropes and mainsails thrumming,
nor-easterly cutting yer bones,
the island emerging to larboard.
We hailed the precious sight.

One shipmate 'd never return,
left under stones in a cove,
wreck-wood across the grave,
reefs groaning, gulls screaming,
black crags cleaving the surf.

None can tell why he picked it,
the Cap'n always a careful man,
atop the cliff with his spyglass,
no fields, not a tree,
nary a lubber on the land,
and us hauling the sea-chests after
cursing the wind and sleet.

Buried 'em?

                I reckon us did.

The map?

                I won't peach.

Another?

                Thank'ee kindly.

Rum…

                it's been meat and drink
                man and wife to me.

HAUNTED VESSELS *

Septimus Goring,
unlikely pioneer,
conjured a ghost ship
that sailed over the horizon
nobody on board.

Rolls Royce and Mitsui's
unmanned drone ships,
sensor and satellite guided,
prowl the seven seas
echoing Marie Celeste.

Four-fingered Septimus
slaughtered the crew,
escaping in a lifeboat;
digitised Navi-tronics
terminates all hands.

BEWARE THE TIME OF NOAH *

Lashing, teeming, bucketing down,
torrents hammer inky slates,
sloshing into gutter seas.

Darkened taxi snouts the waves
to shabby pool of tinkling light –
another for the road?

Dispatched down a lane-way,
sodden memorial blooms
lie spent and wasting.

Good Friday's spring tide
ebbs, sweet-wrappers frothing,
leaky hopes scuppered again.

A periscope scans refugee streets,
convoys of terraces holed in action –
illustrated gables shudder and groan,
going down, all dogs baying.

CONVICTION

A loop of rope with clenched knot,
a blindfold and fusiliers,
a blade above a block,
a hypodermic or cabled seat,
a stake surrounded by logs,
a heap of stones:
the cross.

DIRECTIONS *

Go ye north
one day and one night
with fair wind and full sail
to isles broken by narrow sounds
swarming with sea-fowl.

Beach thyself
turn the boat for shelter
take mussels and sweet-water.
Remain forty months
observe thy vows.

Forget northern raiders
who care only for ale and gold
be as the high sun
who hides a little in the night
and the west wind
who scours the land clean
save for great stones that rear
many hands into the sky.

IN YOUR EYES *

A scattering of islands –
reefs, concealed bays
and exotic vegetation,
strange ecosystems
parted by dangerous channels.

Anglerfish stalk
and molluscs creep
as trenches plunge
into your remote,
protozoan dark.

MESSAGE IN A BOTTLE

Marianne Winkler
      Retired Postal Worker
           found a bottle
               on a beach in Amrum
           the North Frisian Isles
     108 years 4 months
and 18 days after

George Parker Bidder
      Marine Biologist
           threw a bottle
               into the North Sea
        with a message
     in Dutch and German
return to sender
      for the reward
          of one shilling.

Frau Winkler replied to him by post
               at the Marine Biological Association
     Plymouth Devon.

Bidder had died in 1954
      but they sent her many thanks
        and a shilling
            they bought on eBay.

THE OPENING

Ignite

        green

                cowled

lamp

        clasp

                dusty

bundle

        snip

                securing

string

        missives

                flutter

spill

        raise

                steel

blade

        gulp

                corner

incision

        slice

                gummed

edge

        fingers

                hover

quake

        draw

                folded

page

        bring

                to

light

SADDLEWORTH MOOR *

It began with the letter,
or was that the middle,
an end?
No matter.
He takes his pills,
puts on blue corduroys,
cream shirt, cardigan,
makes tea, no toast.

Egg sandwich at Euston,
single, West Coast Express.
Sun glints on sinkholes,
divots, rainwashed trees,
scrawny embankments,
into Piccadilly, platform five.

He turns the letter
through his fingers,
it moistens and bows.
Finally, he is called.
She's sideways to a desk, shakes
his hand, glances at the file,
looks up, speaks, looks away.
He nods, folds the letter,
goes home.

On the mantlepiece, the pictures:
BEA Dakota DC3,
Da uniformed, Ma on arm,
squeezed between the old folks,
baggy suits, floppy hats.
Aldergrove to Ringway in fog,

descending, undercarriage down,
hit the high ground.

City shoes slip and leak,
valley lights gleam.
Hard sedge,
sodden peat.
The last resting place.
First Officer Holt,
Captain Pinkerton,
Radio Officer Haigh,
twenty one passengers
and other lost souls.

THE CLUB

It's exclusive, yet people join every day.
There's no application form,
no interview and no fee.
Enrolment only happens at someone else's behest.
It arrives unexpectedly,
however much you might've prepared.

Resignations are never accepted,
as membership can only be passed
to family and close friends.
Renewals and extensions come along,
whether you're looking for them or not.
The loss club soldiers on,
day by day.

ROGER CURRY

Found in Hereford Bus Station
White pensioner
Slim build
Tall
Grey hair
Stubble
Blue eyes
Squints

American accent
Keeps repeating his name
No memory
No identity papers
Nobody reported
Missing

THE BOSS

Behind his sleek mahogany desk
lie framed diplomas and honours,
an expanse of gilding, signatures and red wax seals
he loves to gesture towards,
sprawling back in a buttoned leather chair
as you remain standing.

All phoney, confides the janitor,
especially one as a fighter pilot in Vietnam –
seizing the joystick, he presses the trigger
and four cannons blaze hot lead,
then he dissolves to a pouting bambino,
waving chubby little arms
and gaping around the cockpit.

THE LAW OF MOTION

Everyone, they say, has a doppelgänger:
neither duplicate, nor clone,
more a strange relative
you never could meet.

When you give to charity
and stuff yourself with cake,
your counterpart steals and starves.

The turning world
will always fetch
another side.

DEAR SIR OR MADAM

Please forgive this intrusion
I folded your new tablecloth
stiff and cool
and I had to write.
Be most assured I do not ask for favour
nor indeed for money
though heaven knows our times are hard as the frost
that grasped my throat as I trod to work today
the sun's low beams striking the mist
above the bleach green.
Gentle sir or madam
I do not wish to trouble your comfort at breakfast
whether partridge
smoked herring
or a brace of bantam's eggs
but I implore you
hear me out.

I am a lapper
have been these dozen years
since father passed
a position I gained as a lass
that detains me for most of God's hours
six days of the week
and puts bread into hungry mouths.
I will not presume upon your knowing
the complexity of this trade
suffice it to say that mine are the last
of many hands which turn humble flax
into the fine cloth that spreads before you.
I have heard it said that linen
fashioned by our hands

graces the finest tables
from Chittagong to Valparaiso.
Truly does the sun ever set upon our works?

Kind sir or madam
I must not burden your patience
any further
I am an honest God-fearing woman
and I ask this
will you raise a prayer
for the labouring poor of the parish?

Your faithful servant in the lapping room.

READING THE BROCHURE OF FARROW & BALL, I UPDATE THEIR RANGE OF COLOURS

Smoked Trout
Blazer
Oxford Stone
Dog End
Croquet
Payday Loan

Pale Hound
Thoroughbred
Rectory Green
Food Bank
Forelock
Bended Knee

White Tie
Tiffin
Elephant's Back
Rent Arrears
Heirloom
Bailiff's Knock

Satin Slipper
Soirée
Pied à Terre
Cold Shoulder
Ebony
Workhouse Door

GRAVEYARD CLOSED DUE TO COVID-19 LOCKDOWN *

Priests, undertakers and mourners
barred until further notice.
Gatherings of two or more
ghouls will be dispersed.
Zombies without sanitizer
or hands are forbidden,
likewise the undead –
whether or not taking
essential exercise.
For their own safety,
the previously buried
are respectfully requested
to remain interred.

CRITIQUE

Brandishing a serrated knife,
John Paul Mulready
bursts into the flat above
and pounces on Dermot Byrne –
biting his nose and ear,
stabbing him in the leg.

Mulready attacks Byrne
for always reciting poetry.
Guilty, he declares.
With 116 previous convictions,
he's jailed in Dublin
for two and a half years.

DEAR READER, I MURDERED HIM *
— *for Ian Rankin*

Heaving bosoms…
      a child abused,
the tall, dark stranger…
      a fugitive from justice,
every breathless encounter…
      a padded cell
in the maximum security wing,

where romantic novelists,
      stranglers
and machete-artistes,
      scrawl birthday-card ditties
for phone time and snout,
      under rehab
with the guild of the golden dagger.

BUZZ LIGHTYEAR *

Samuel Stephens
changed his name by deed poll,
opened new bank accounts,
continued his career
as a business manager
and raised funds
for a cancer charity.

Applying to renew his driving license,
he was refused.
Issuing a license
to a fictional character
would bring DVLA into disrepute.
Buzz appealed and won.

BONNIE, LUKE, GRACE & CHARLIE

Pool their pocket-money,
load Mum & Dad's car
with fishing rods and crisps,
run away at midnight,
drive hundreds of miles
past wallabies and sheep farms,
refuel at a lonely station
as the sun climbs over gum trees
shining the way to Sydney.

Armed police block the road,
drag the kids from the car,
frisk and handcuff them.
Their parents reported it
stolen.

WAYS TO KILL A PRESIDENT *

Sniper
Grenade
Car Bomb
Exploding Lectern
Lethal Milkshake
Infected Diving Suit
Cyanide Cocktail
Poisoned Shoes

Femme Fatale
Toxic Fountain Pen
Infected Aerosol
Arsenic Ice-Cream
Exploding Cigar
Old Age

THE CROSSING *
— for Philippe Petit

Between two fluttering candles
the swallowtail dances –
a lucent tightrope of guile,
balance and pixie dust.
On fire, but not burnt.

SERGEANT SILVERBACK

Fresh fruit breakfast,
a peck and a hug –
boards the 07.15
in furry suit
and black mask,
sidles to his seat,
commuters peek
and look away.

Knuckles to the ground,
he lumbers marathons
to protect great apes.
He roars at mileposts,
climbs Big Ben with a damsel
to swat planes.

GARFIELDING *

If beachcombers could be arsed,
after lasagne and ice cream,
to wander into Iroise,
trudge coves and white sands,
they'd see dolphins, otters, grey seals
and a crouching orange tabby,
handset on his back,
whose eyes spring open
as you raise the phone
to tell the song of the sea –
midwinter storms,
lost cargo containers,
and six thousand replicas
poisonously alive.

WATERSHED

Gushing between glaciers
and the ocean bed,
a vast, unremitting tide
sculpts the reluctant land
as the moment needs,
sweeping particles for sediment
or in raging spate, whole trees.

Pulled from the awkward bank,
undertows twist and swirl us
beyond the shallows.
You roar onwards
in sleek rolling waves,
plunging deep and dangerous
into the cascade.

TELLING THE BEES *

No
       flummer, fibs, waffle,
blather, rattle, hype,
       hearsay, palaver,
witter, wind, yap,
       soft-soap, prattle,
scams, clack, twaddle,
       garden-path jabber,
noise, fakery, bull,
       tittle-tattle, cackle,
piffle, porkies, gab,
       fairytales, gibber,
bluff, fudges, babble,
       flimflam or blah.
Truth.

NOTES

The notes follow the sequence in which the poems appear in the book. I have only provided a note where I felt it was required.

Compass
The poem refers to Unst, the most northerly of the Shetland Islands and a future satellite launch site for the UK Space Agency.

Writing Exercises
Parchment, made from animal skins in a slow and complex process, was the primary writing material in Europe for over 6000 years.

East Ireland: A Colonial Notebook
The military men who wrote of their exploits in the Journals of the Ordnance Survey of Ireland and the Journals of the East India Company were cut from the very same cloth. The narrative is invented.

Flat White
'Homeless man found dead in coffee-shop' was the news story that led to this poem.

Counting on Chance
After the mystery benefactor of Blackhall Colliery.

Pilgrim
After 'Shattered Lives', a Concern Worldwide report on child refugees from the war in Syria.

Breakfast in Kutupalong
A temporary camp in Bangladesh with a million Rohingya refugees. It is by far the biggest refugee camp in the world. The poem was written for Concern Worldwide and was used as part of their campaign to mark the two year anniversary of the Rohingya crisis.

Reckoning
After an exhibition of the work of the Inquisition in Münster, Germany, during the 16th Century. Since then, St Lambert's Church in Münster has kept three iron cages on its spire in commemoration.

The Prophet
A French evangelical visits the Canary Islands.

Chuan-pu
The nickname for Donald Trump in China.

The Romanovs
In 2017 a Russian oligarch sought to re-establish the Romanov Empire on a Pacific island he'd bought, declaring himself Prime Minister.

Fixer
Where photography meets criminality.

Visit Nagasaki
Whilst Japan was a closed society, this port city was open to the world. Hibakusha are survivors of the atom bombs. Their testimonies have been recorded and can be heard by visitors to Nagasaki and Hiroshima.

Bog Men
The well preserved bodies of two men were found in Meath

and Offaly, Ireland, in 2003. They had been ritually killed and buried in bogs around 2300 years ago.

Curtain Boar
A beast that has lost interest in sex, rendering it of no use to a pig farmer. It would be sent to the abattoir.

The Harpsichord Tuner
Ludwig van Beethoven was born on 16 December 1770. His genome was sequenced in 2023 from an authenticated lock of hair. This showed that his Y-chromosome was quite different to that of the male line of Beethovens from the 15th Century to the present day. This means that Ludwig's father was not a Beethoven.

Albie's Phantom
Justice Albie Sachs is a South African lawyer and anti-apartheid activist. In 1988 he lost an arm and an eye in a car bomb planted by a Government agent. He later became one of the architects of the new Constitution for South Africa, under the presidency of Nelson Mandela.

Habana Cabaret
Most Cubans are descended from slaves. US sanctions, in place since 1958, have led to much hardship. Reggaeton is Latin American rap music. Jinetero /Jinetera (literally a jockey) is Cuban slang for a hustler (male/female).

Baggage
26 million pieces of luggage went missing on international flights in 2022.

The Knowledge
Artefacts show that different groups of early humans intermingled and spread across Europe over many thousands of years. Social learning is believed to have been a crucial part

of this process.

Saga

After a visit to the Orkney Islands, which were ruled by Viking Earls from the 9ᵗʰ to the 15ᵗʰ Century. The names in the poem are on record but the narrative is invented.

Passage

Dedicated to the fourteen villagers from Addergoole, Mayo, Ireland, who travelled on the maiden voyage of RMS Titanic. Only three survived.

Customs

The Northern Ireland / Republic of Ireland border is 310 miles long and cuts through many homes and villages.

Concerning the first voyage of R L Stevenson with his father

In 1869 Thomas Stevenson took his teenage son on a voyage to Orkney and Shetland to encourage him to join the family business, lighthouse building. As we know, Robert Louis became a writer. 'Treasure Island' was his first novel, and the map of the island in the book bears a strong resemblance to Unst, the most northerly of the Shetlands.

Haunted Vessels

Septimus Goring is a character in the first publication of Sir Arthur Conan Doyle, which dramatised the true story of the ship Maria Celeste, found abandoned in 1872. Conan Doyle's story (published anonymously) was taken by many to be a first-hand account of the mystery, and the name he gave the ship is the one that has endured.

Beware the Time of Noah

After a stark message nailed to a tree near Belfast.

Directions
Written on Papa Westray, one of the smallest and remotest of the Orkney Islands. The Norse word 'papa', meaning monk or priest, is a common island name in Orkney, Shetland and the Outer Hebrides.

In Your Eyes
A scary self-promoter on YouTube.

Saddleworth Moor
Dedicated to the unknown man found dead on the moor in 2015.

Graveyard Closed due to Covid-19 Lockdown
After a notice from the Town Council attached to the newly-padlocked gate of my local cemetery in April 2020. Gallows humour is widespread among Medical and Emergency Services personnel; it helps them to cope with the intense stress of their working lives.

Dear Reader, I Murdered Him
After Ian Rankin's appearance on Desert Island Discs. He described writing as 'therapeutic' and 'exorcising your demons'. Then added, 'That's why most crime writers are actually well-balanced individuals. We get all the dark stuff out on the page. It's the romance writers you've got to watch out for.' I sent the poem to Ian, via his publisher. Ian wrote back telling me it was the first time he'd had a poem dedicated to him.

Buzz Lightyear
The UK's Driver and Vehicle Licensing Agency is a notoriously impenetrable Government body.

Ways to Kill a President
After 'Executive Action: 634 Ways to Kill Castro' by Fabian Escalante, in which the ex-head of the Cuban Secret Service details the many attempts the CIA made to assassinate Fidel Castro.

The Crossing
Philippe Petit is a French performance artist who specialises in unauthorised high-wire walks across prominent buildings, such as the Cathedral of Notre-Dame de Paris. His crossing of the twin towers of New York's World Trade Centre was the subject of a film 'Man on Wire', directed by James Marsh.

Garfielding
Iroise is a Marine Nature Reserve in Brittany, France, where thousands of plastic Garfield telephones have washed ashore.

Telling the Bees
An ancient custom requires the head of the household to tell their bees of any significant changes in the family and village. Failure to keep the bees clearly informed was believed to result in the loss or death of the colony.

ACKNOWLEDGEMENTS

I should like to thank the editors of the following publications, where a number of the poems in this collection first appeared.

The Blue Nib, Bluepepper, Carillon, Drawn to the Light, Find, The Galway Review, The Haibun Journal, Heartland, The Honest Ulsterman, Ink, Sweat & Tears, The Interpreter's House, Latch, Magma, Markings, Matter, Militant Thistles, Not Dark Yet, Poetry Ireland Review, Poetry Salzburg Review, The Poets' Republic, The Recusant, The Riverbank Review, Rush, The Stare's Nest, Stop the World, Tales from the Forest, Tamara, The Trees of Kilbroney Park, Where My River Flows, What the Peacock Replied.

I am grateful to Dempsey & Windle Publishing for permission to reprint a number of poems from *The Skylark's Call.*

I should also like to thank the judges of the following poetry competitions, where a number of the poems in this collection have won awards.

Seamus Burns Creative Writing Competition (2019)
Billy Collins Masterclass Competition (2019)
Writing Armistice Poetry Competition (2018)
York Literature Festival Poetry Competition (2018)
Gregory O'Donoghue International Poetry Competition (2018)
Allingham Poetry Competition (2017)
Mere Literary Festival Poetry Competition (2017)
Cannon Poets Sonnet Competition (2017)

Rush Poetry Competition (2017)
Federation of Writers, Scotland, Poetry Competition (2016)
Artists Embassy International Poetry Contest (2016)
Doolin Writers Festival Poetry Award (2016)
Atlanta Review International Poetry Competition (2015)
Slipstream Poetry Competition (2015)
Torbay Open Poetry Competition (2015)

And finally, I wish to thank BSPG.